PAYSAGES FASCINANTS

Livre de coloriage pour se détendre et soulager le stress

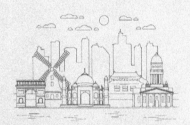
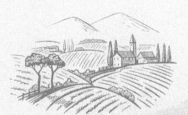

Nature & Art Editions

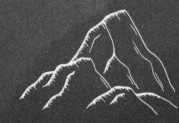

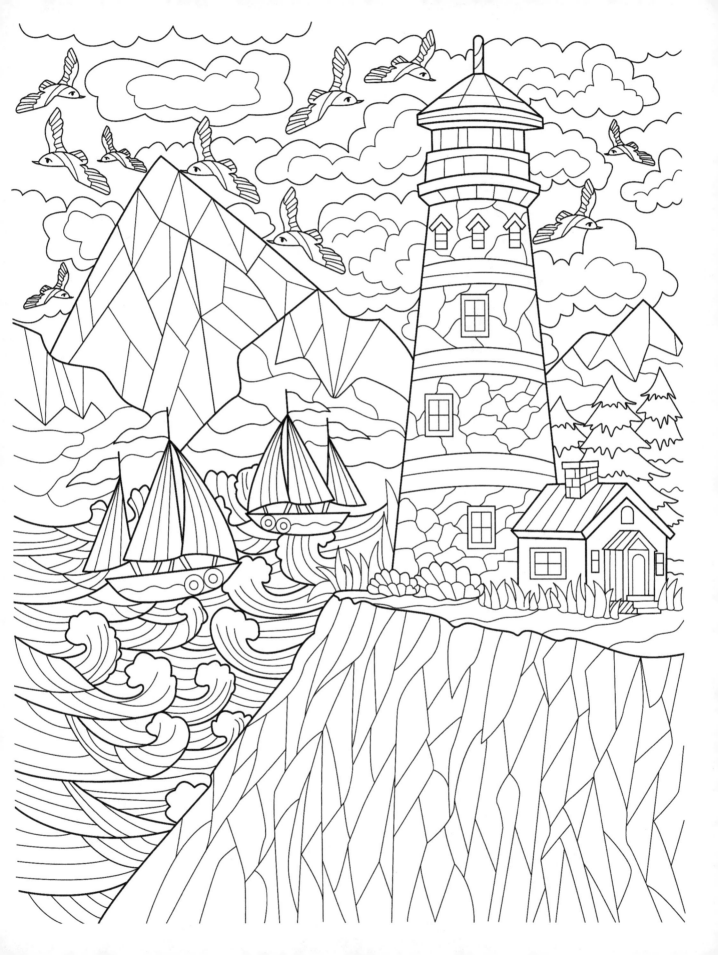

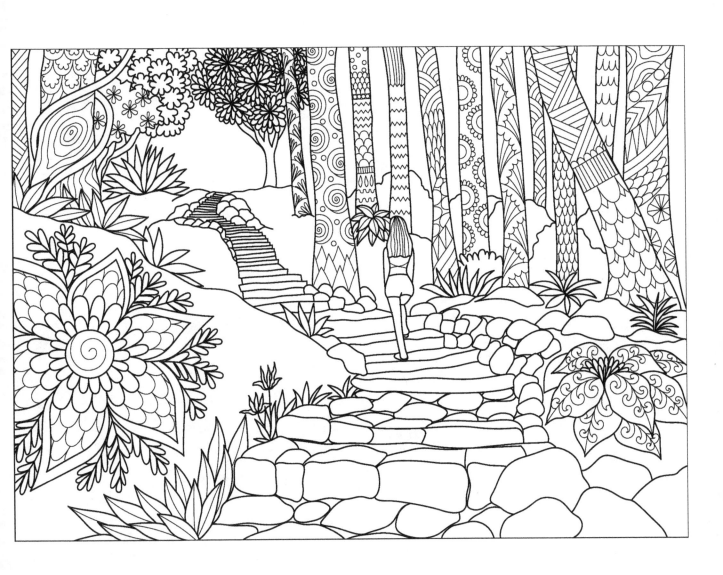

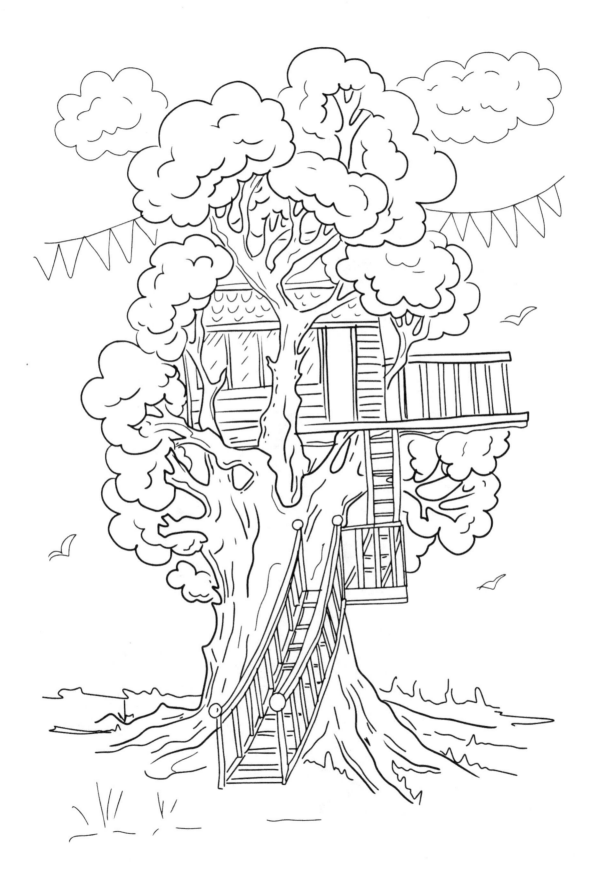

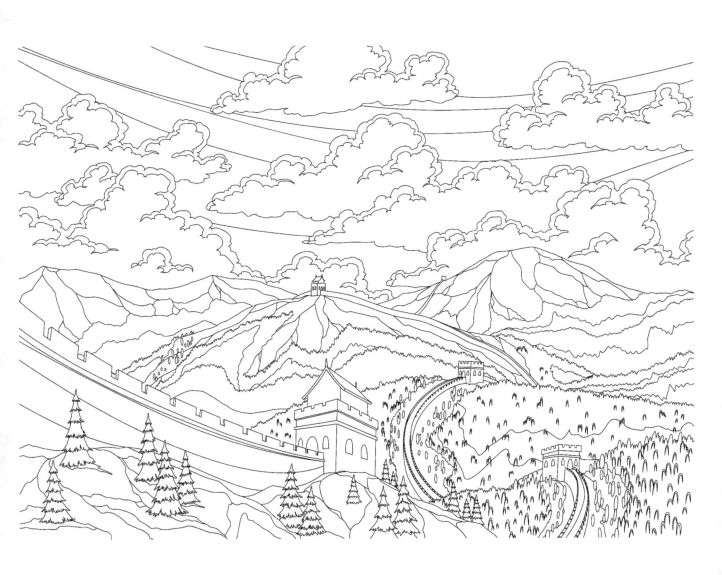

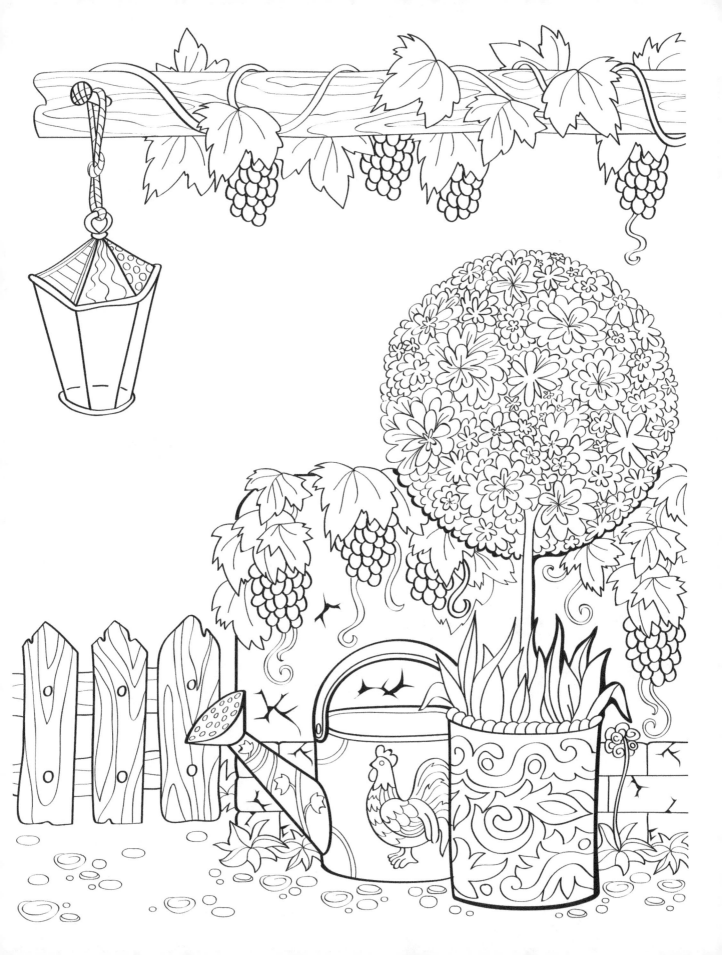

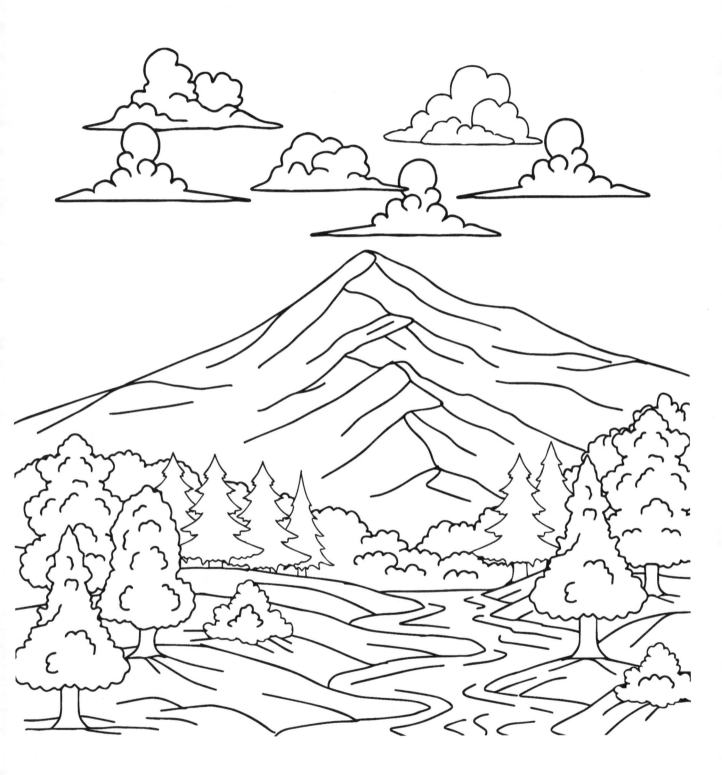

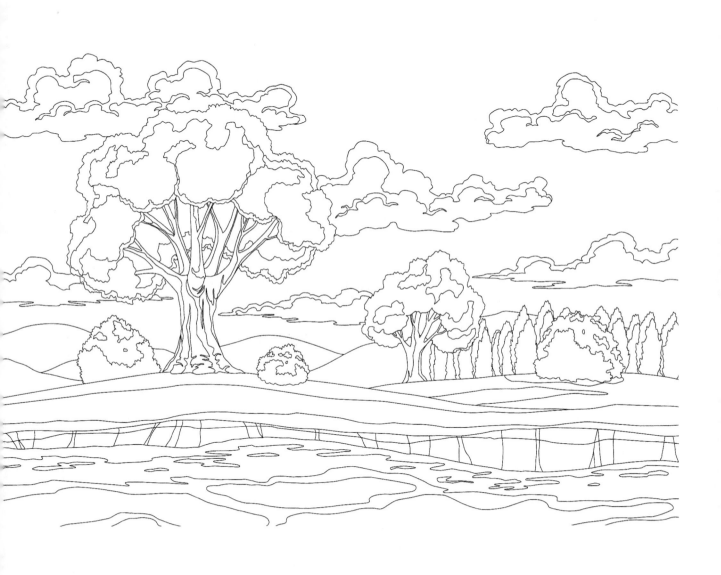

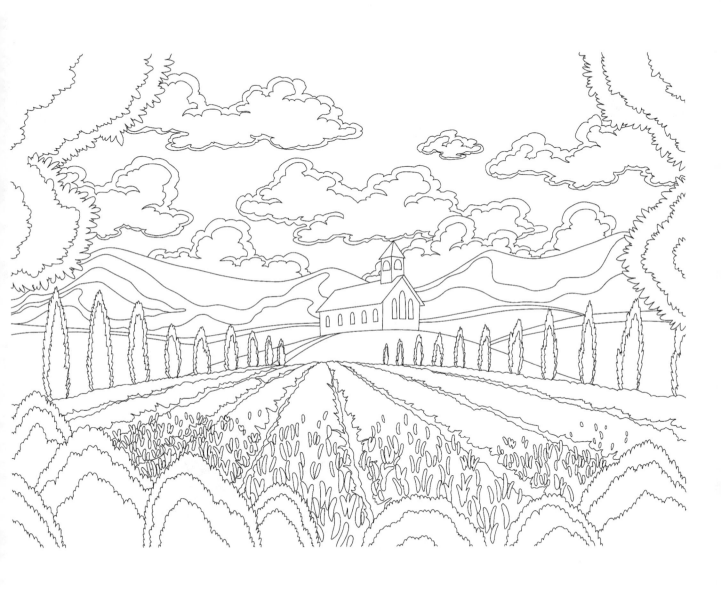

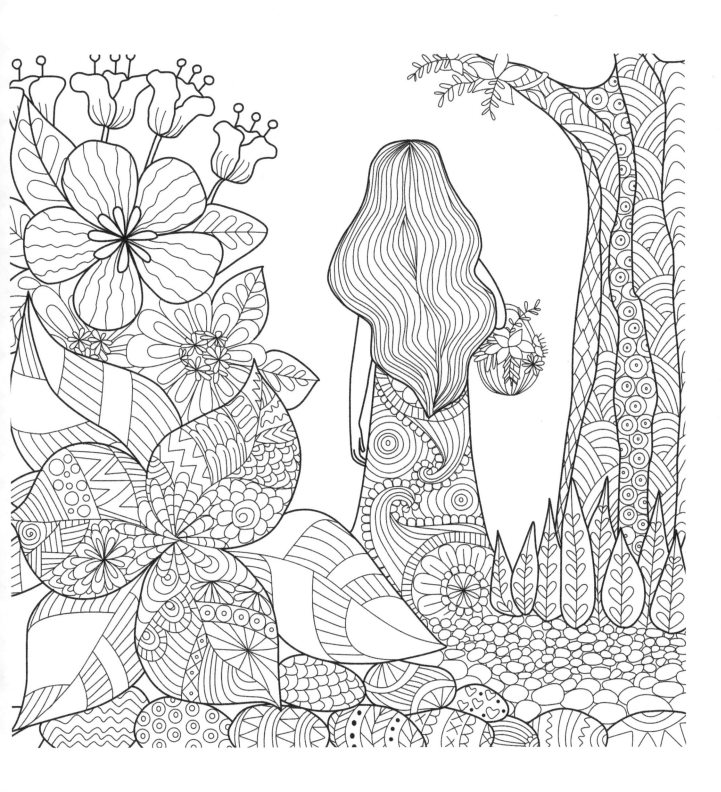

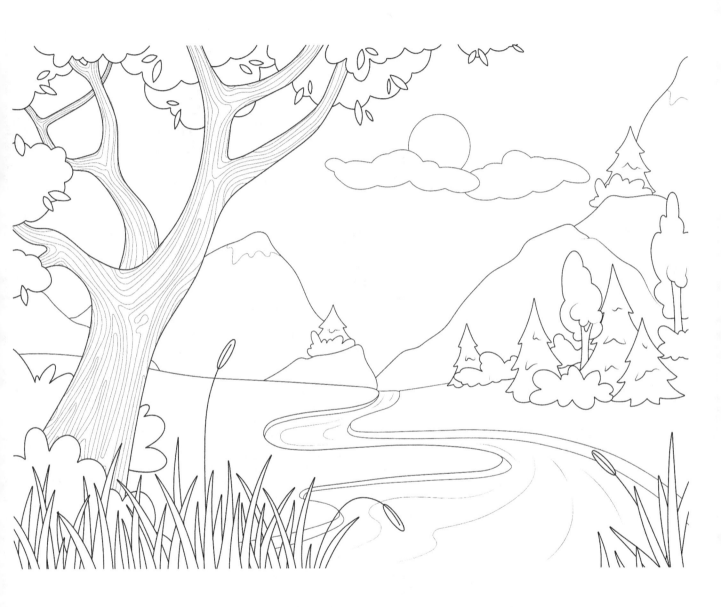

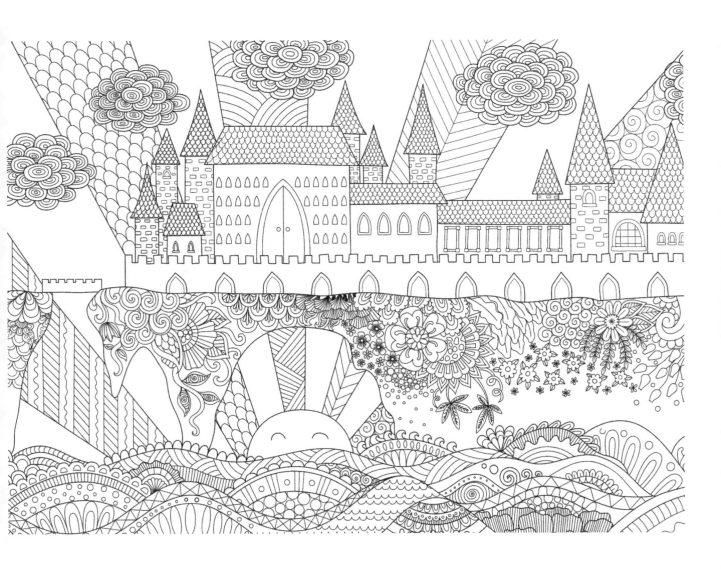

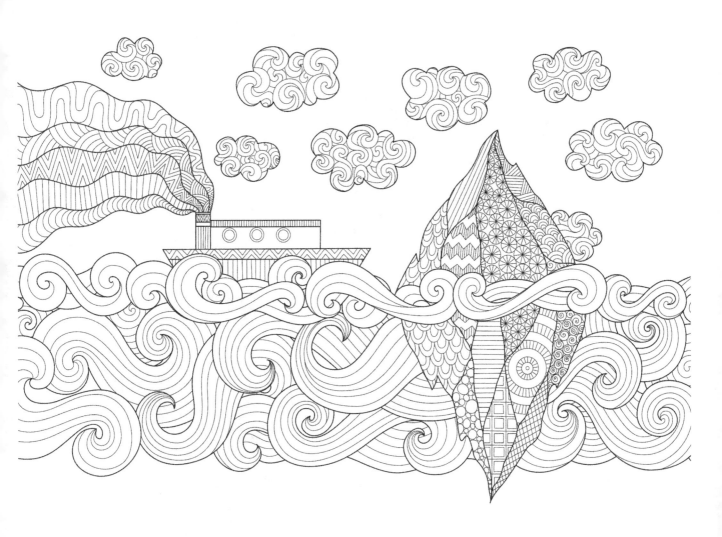

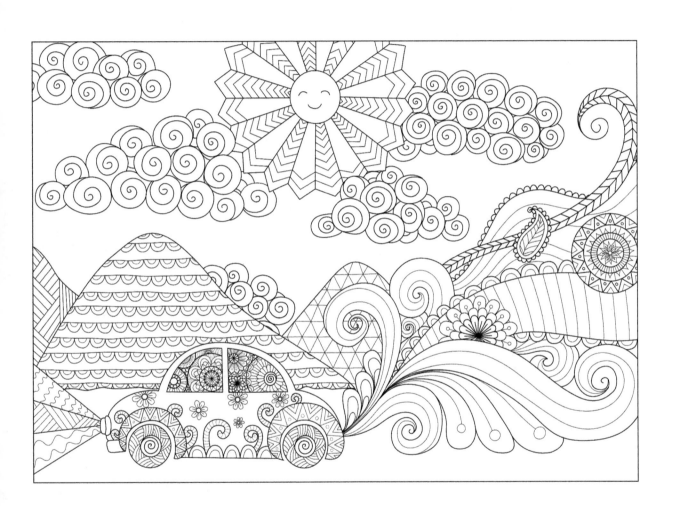

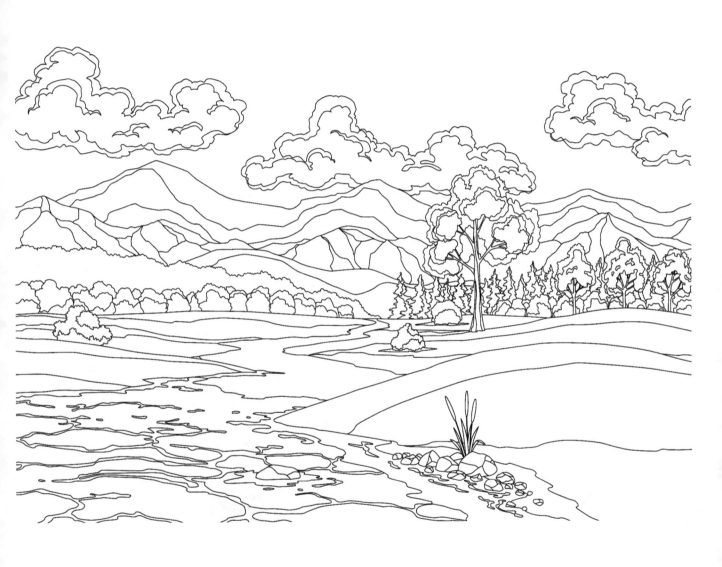

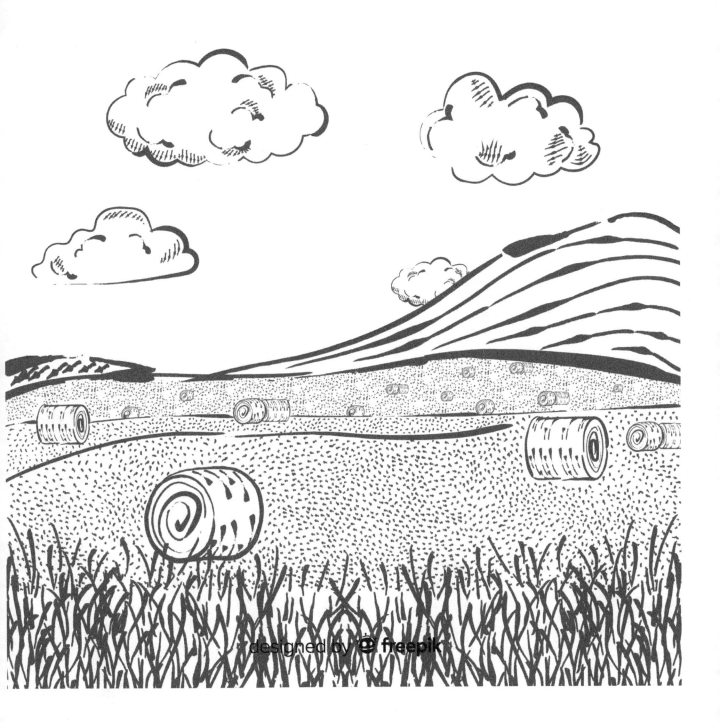

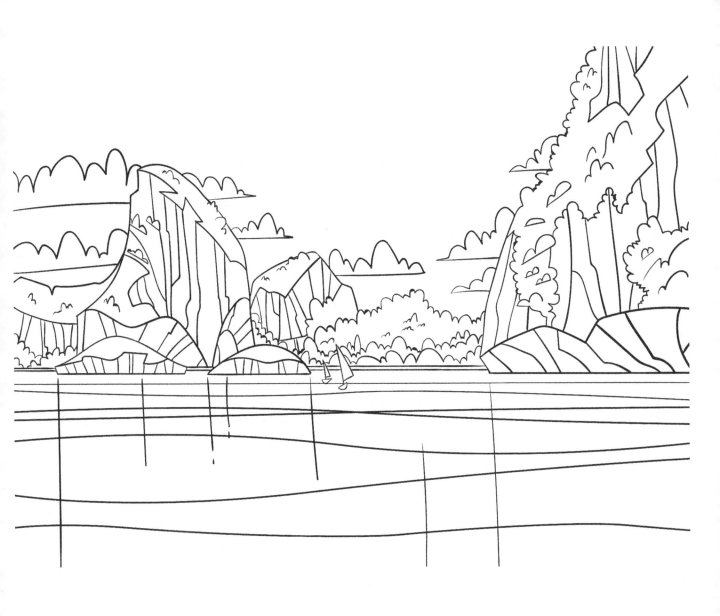

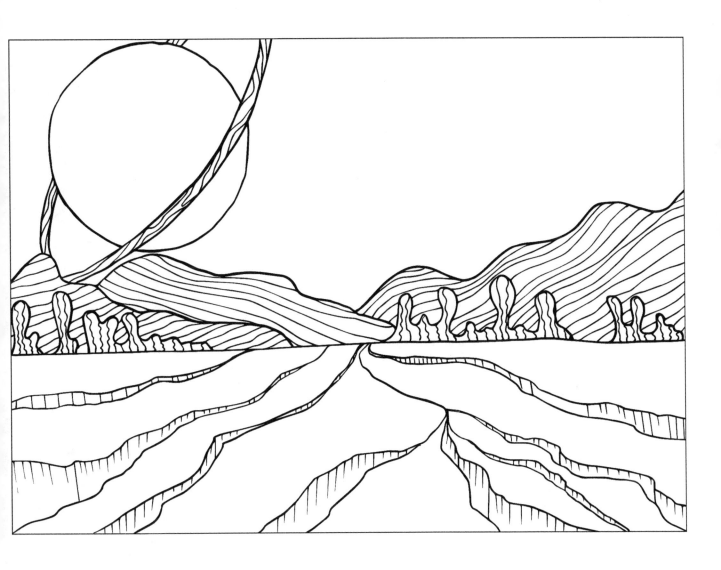

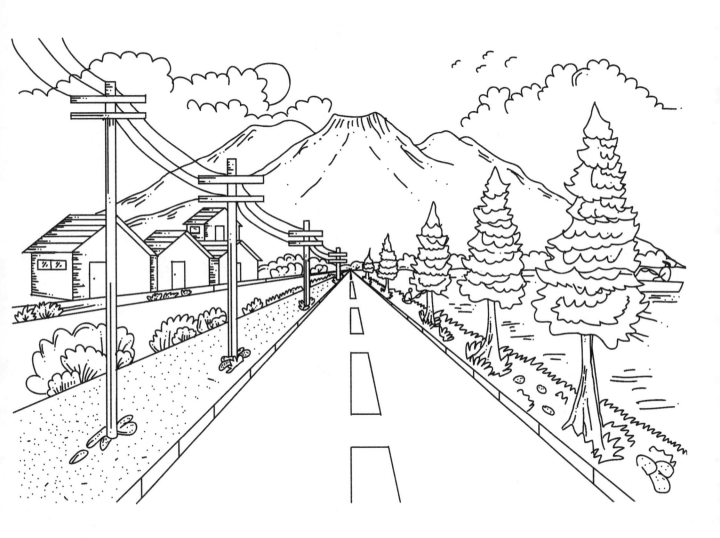

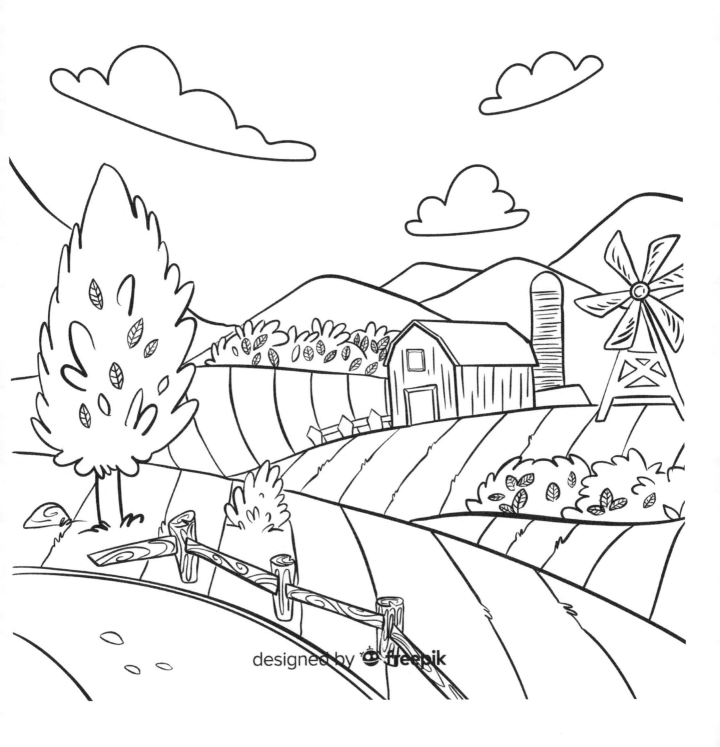

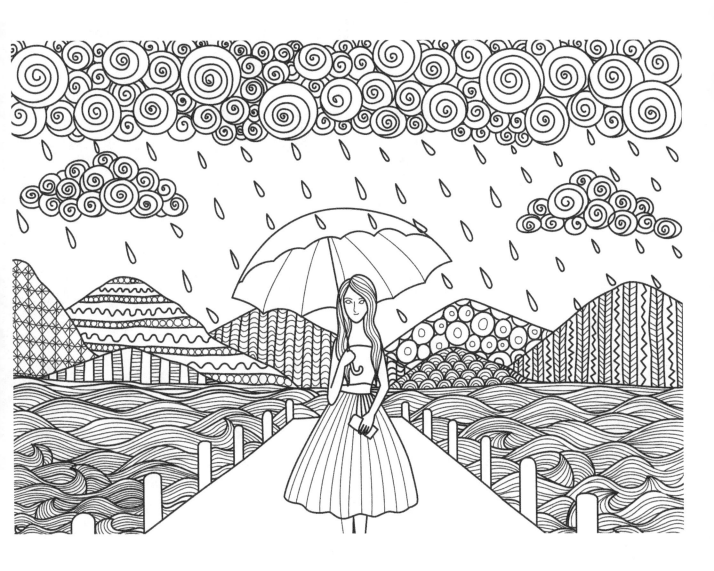

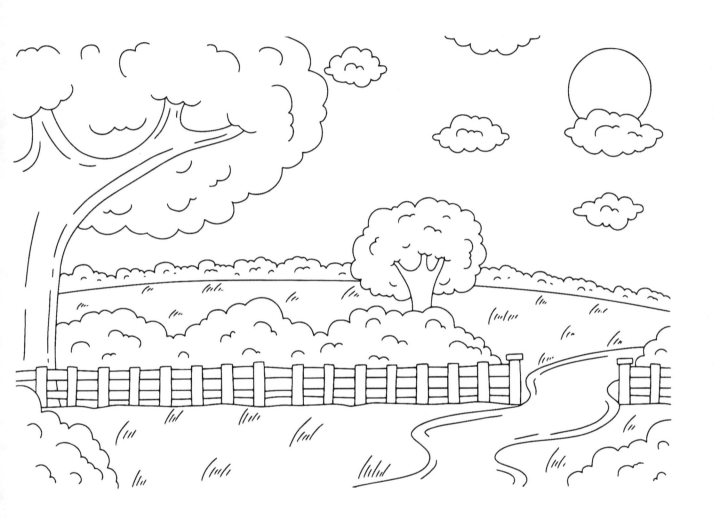

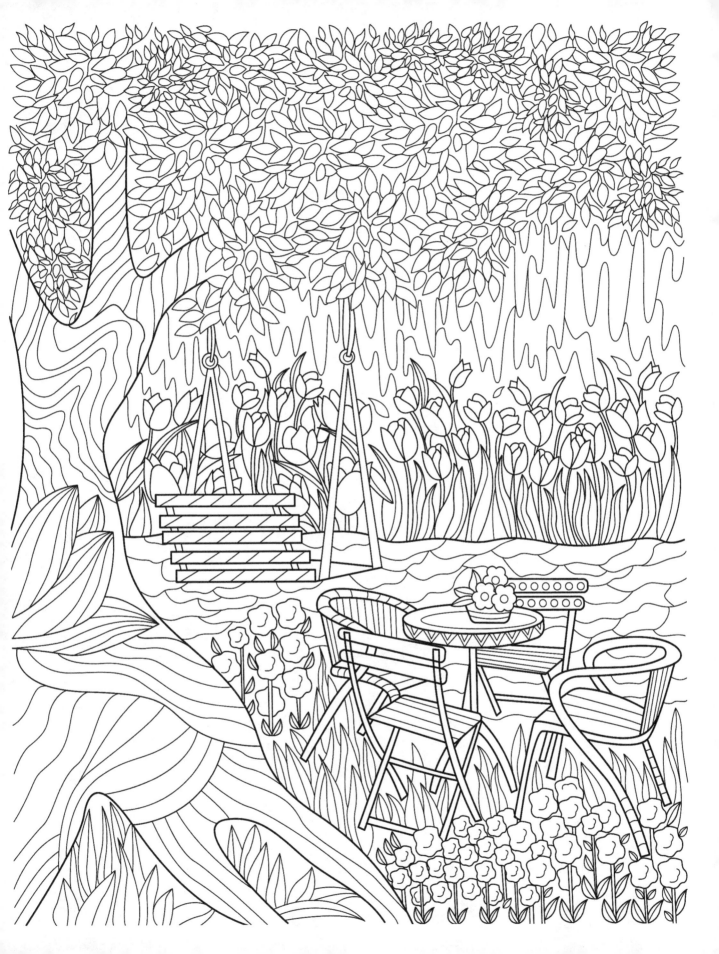

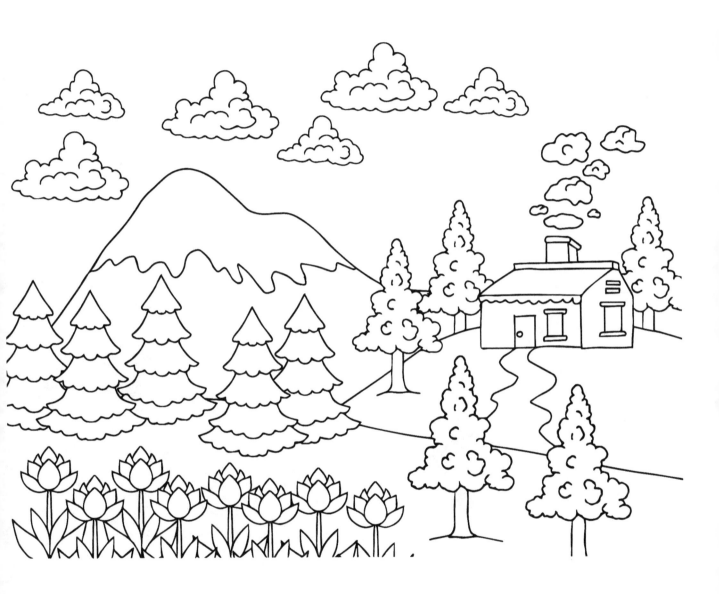

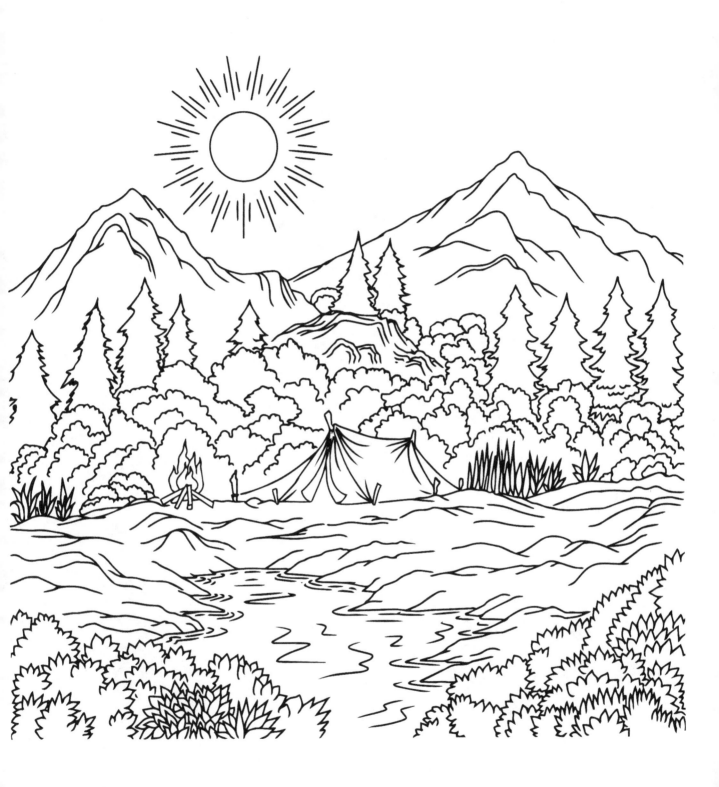

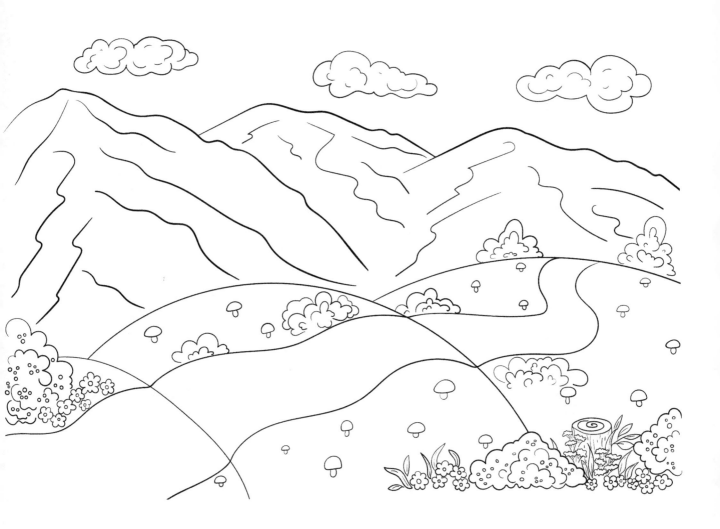

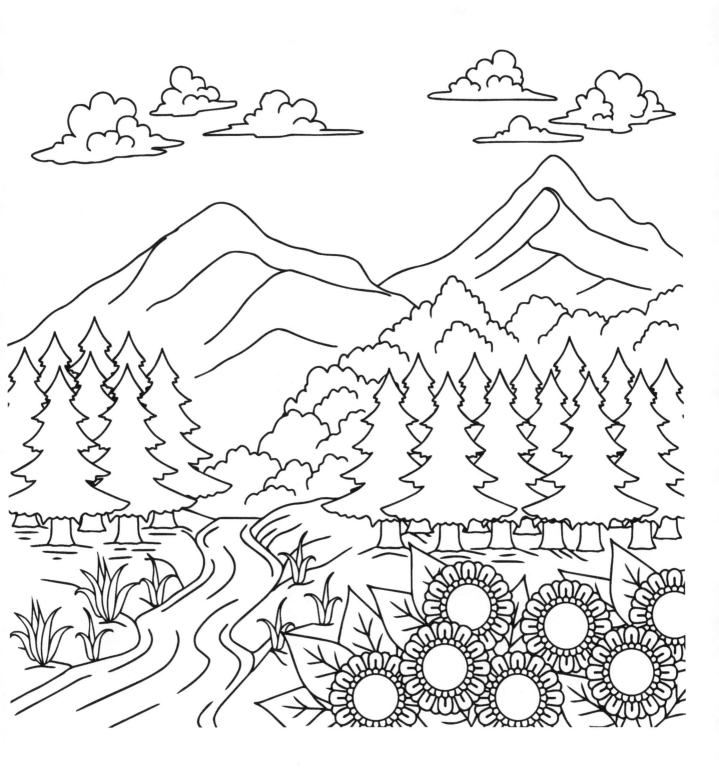

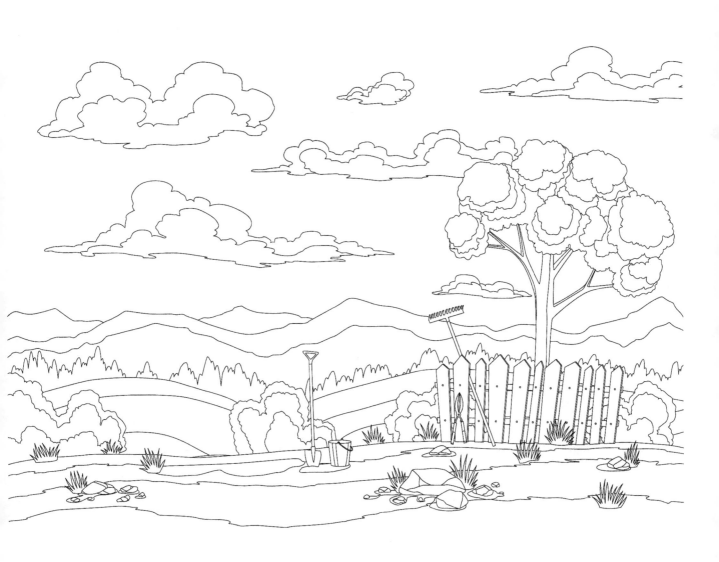

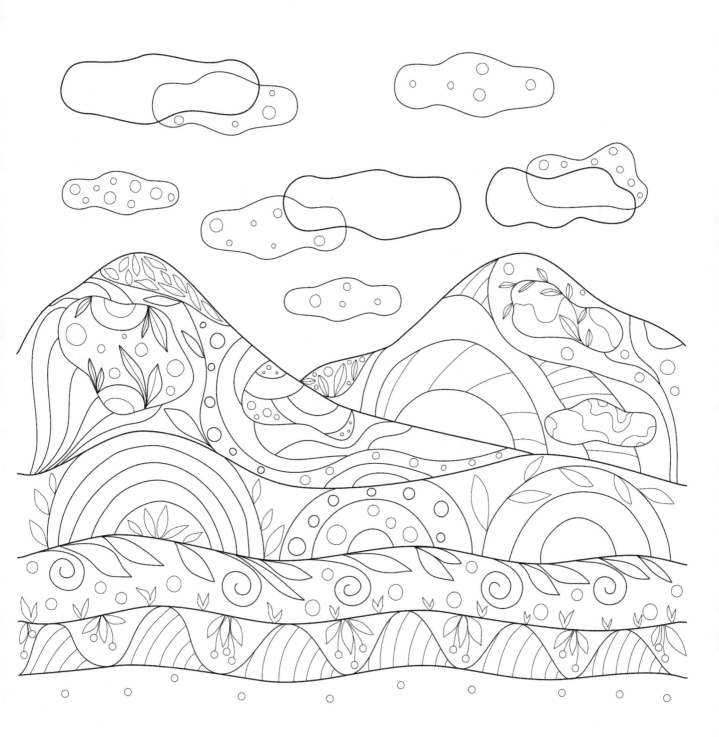

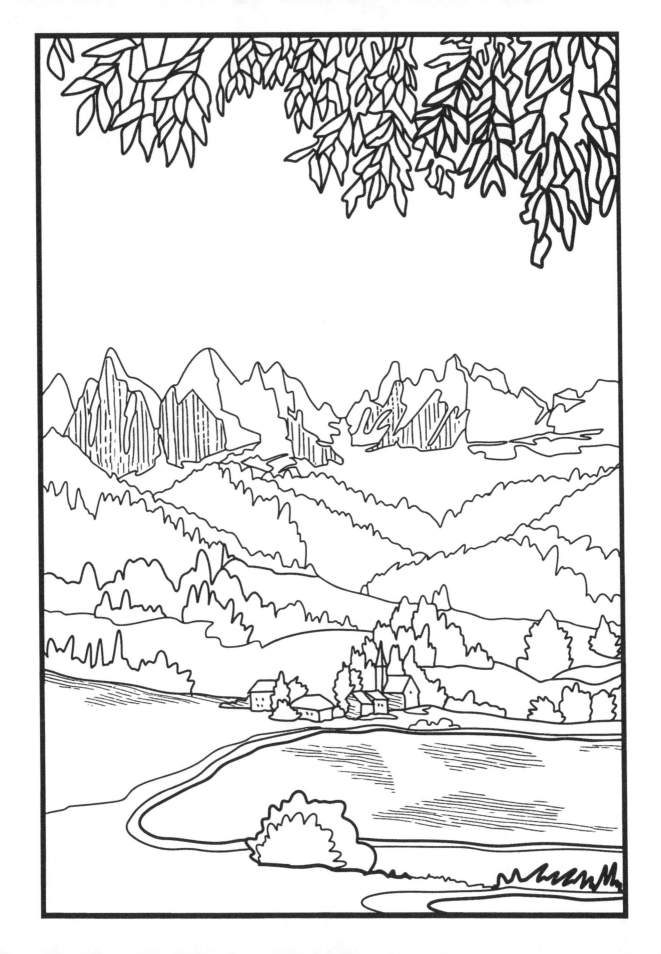

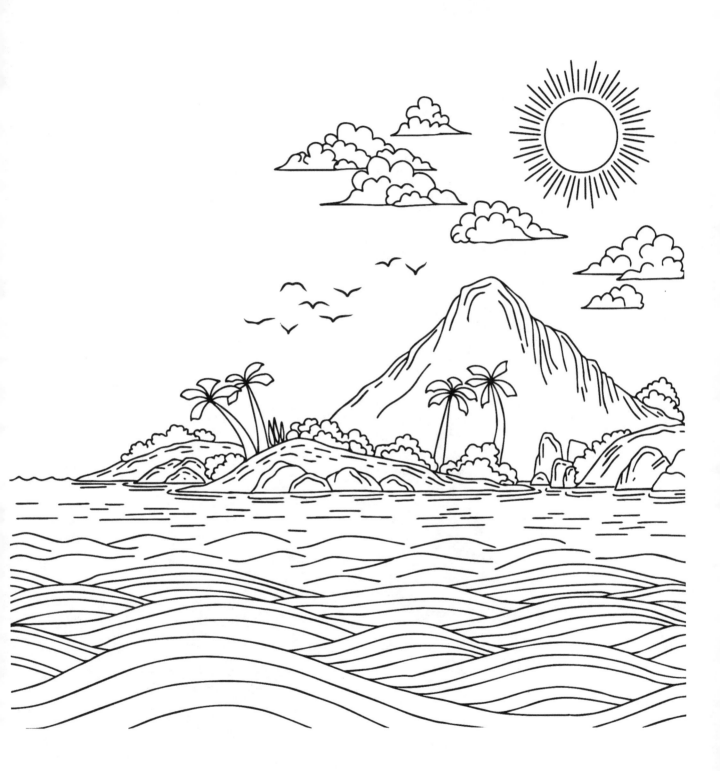

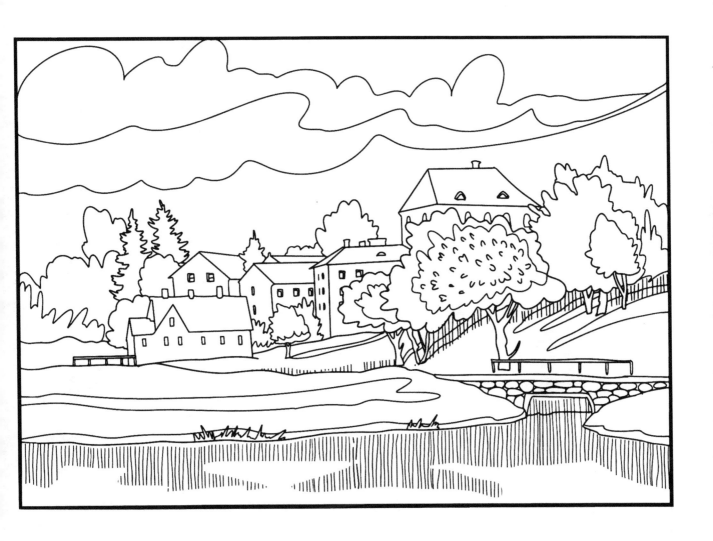

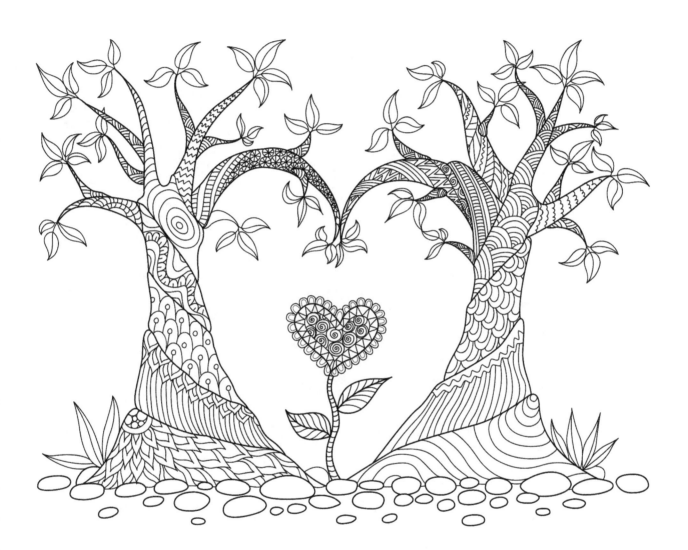

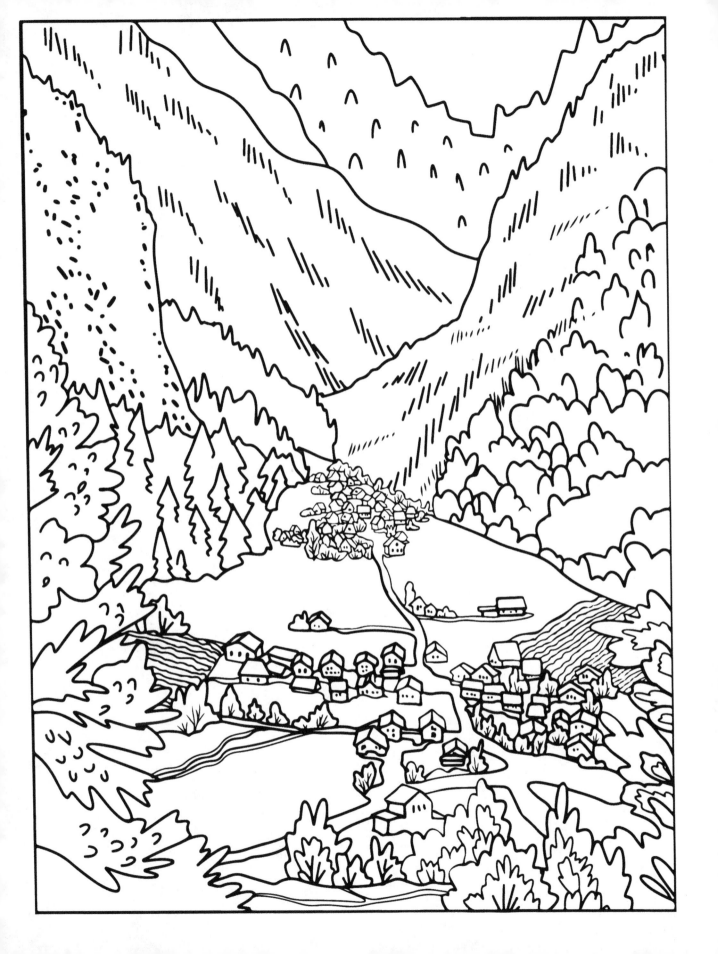

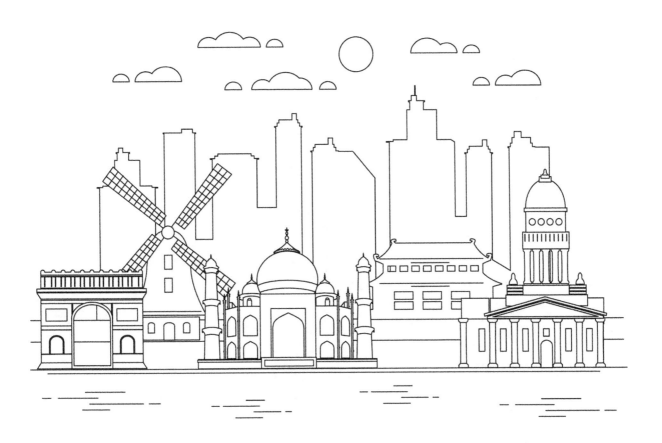

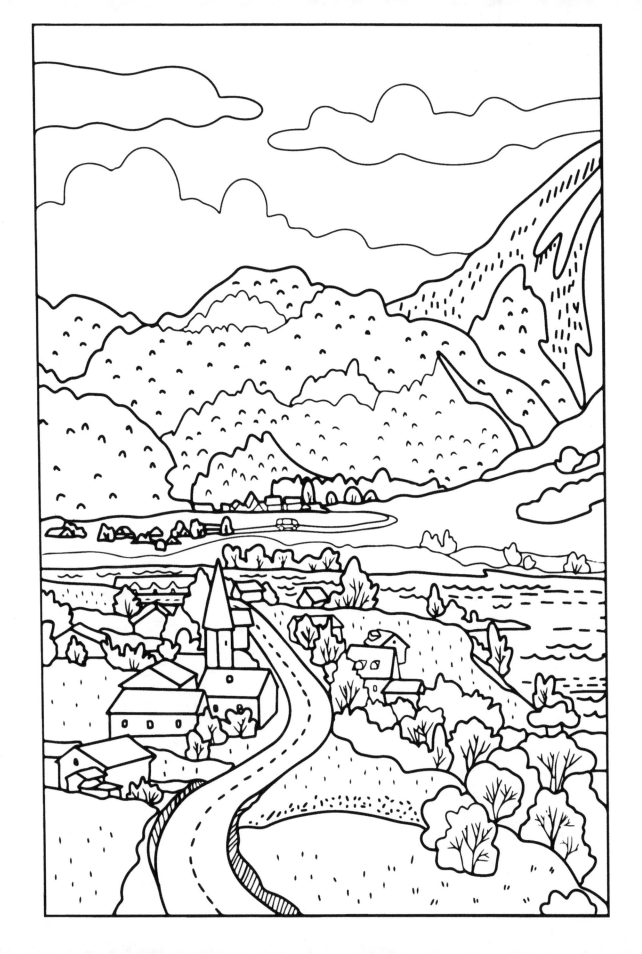

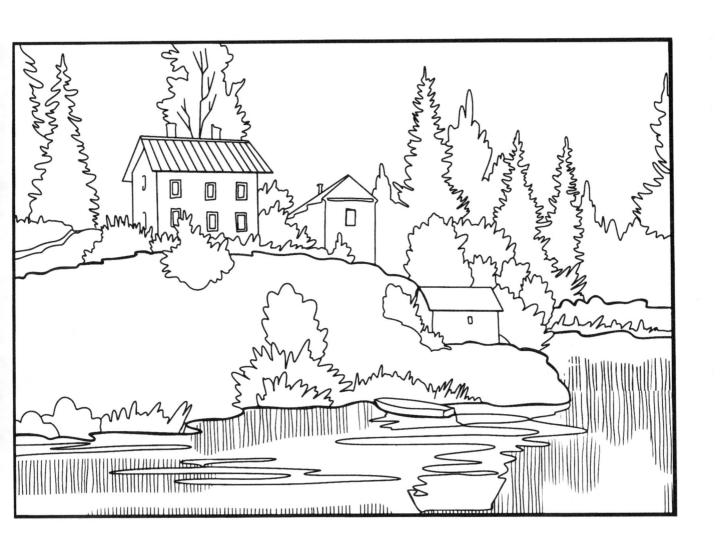

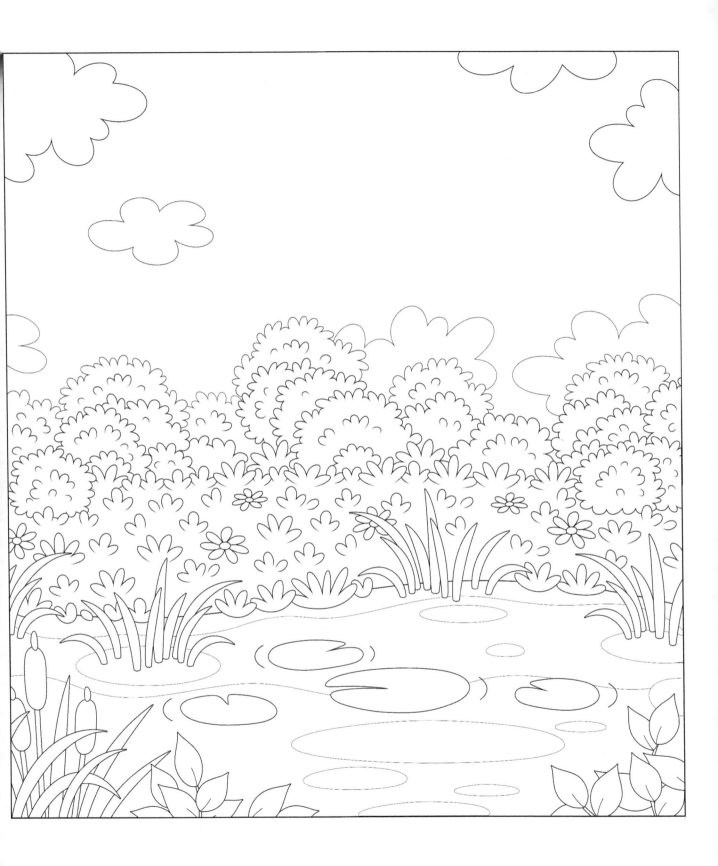

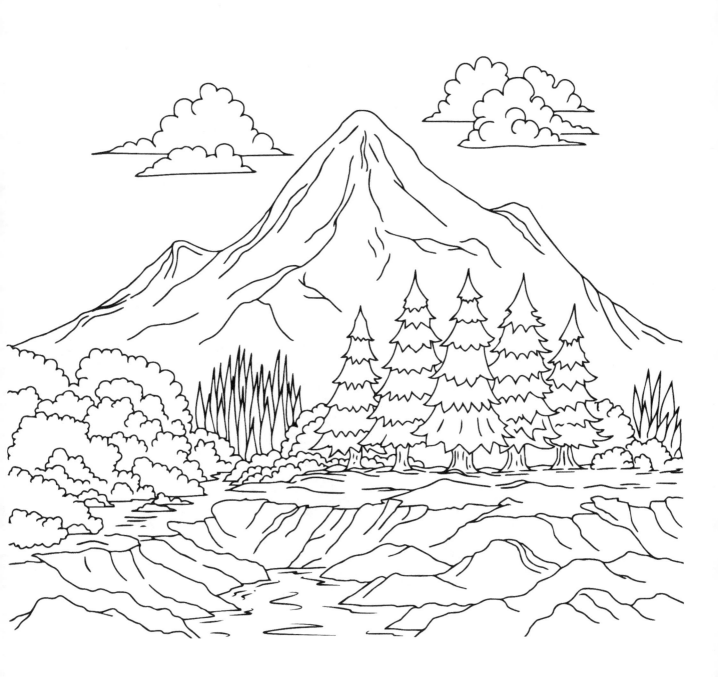

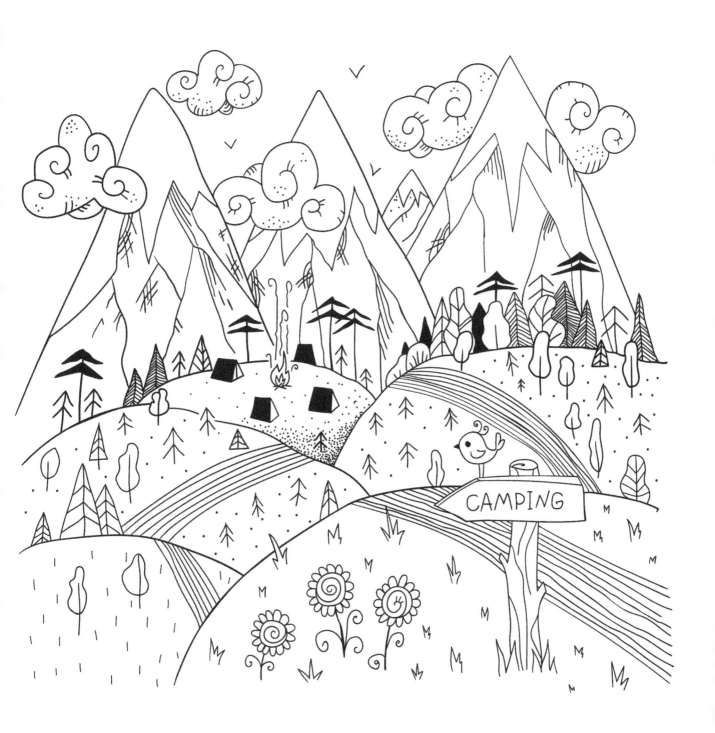

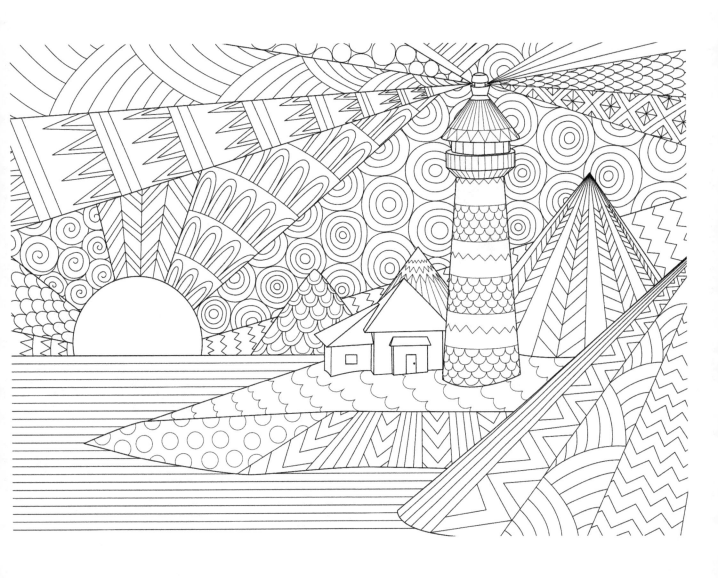

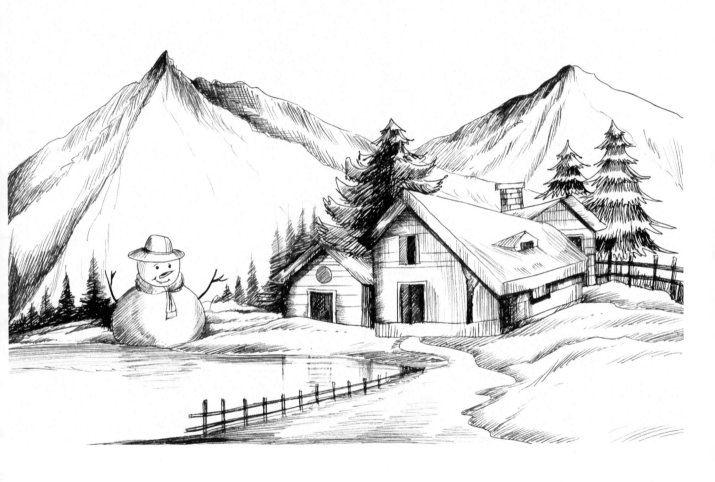

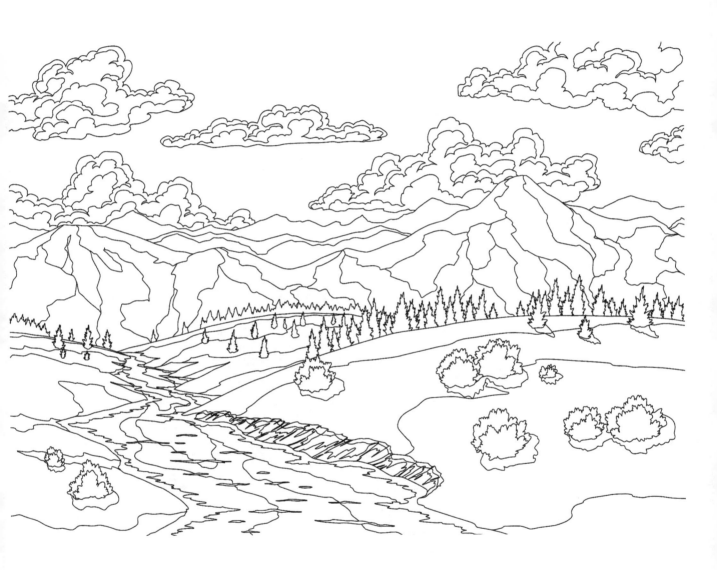

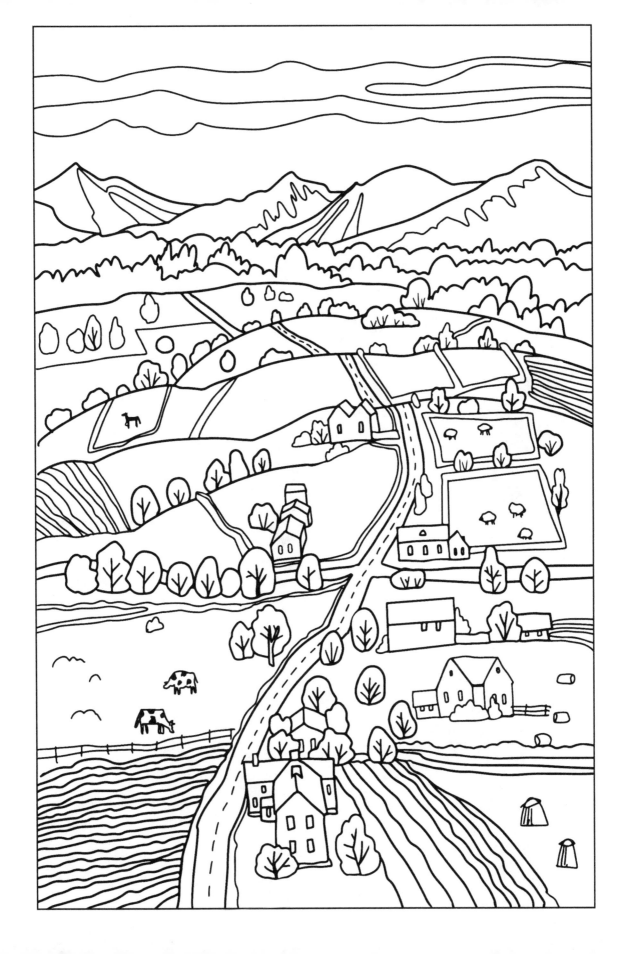

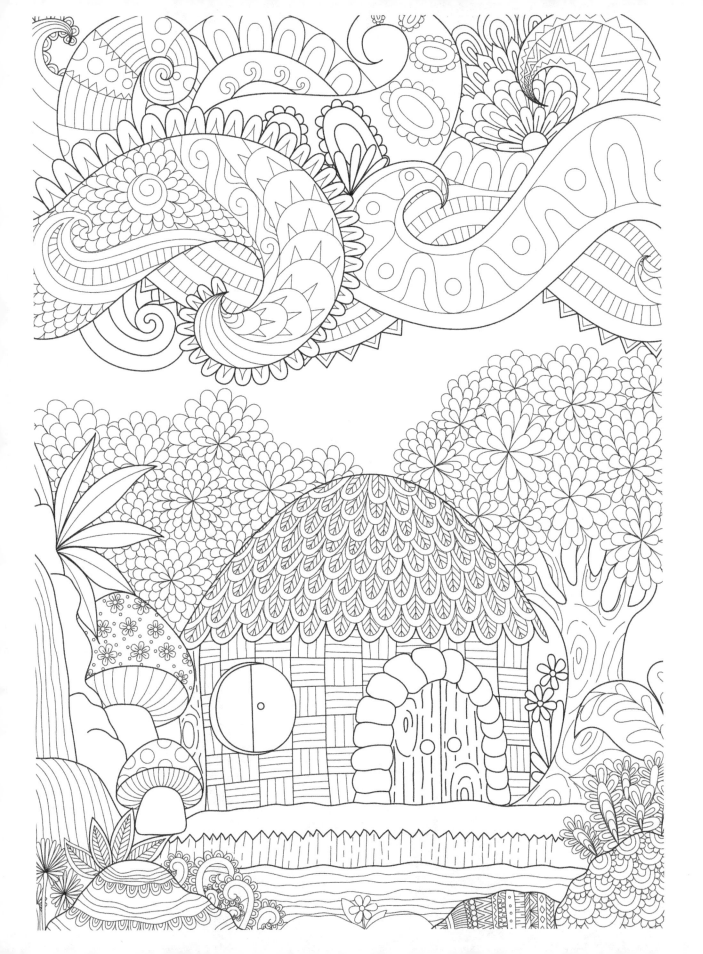

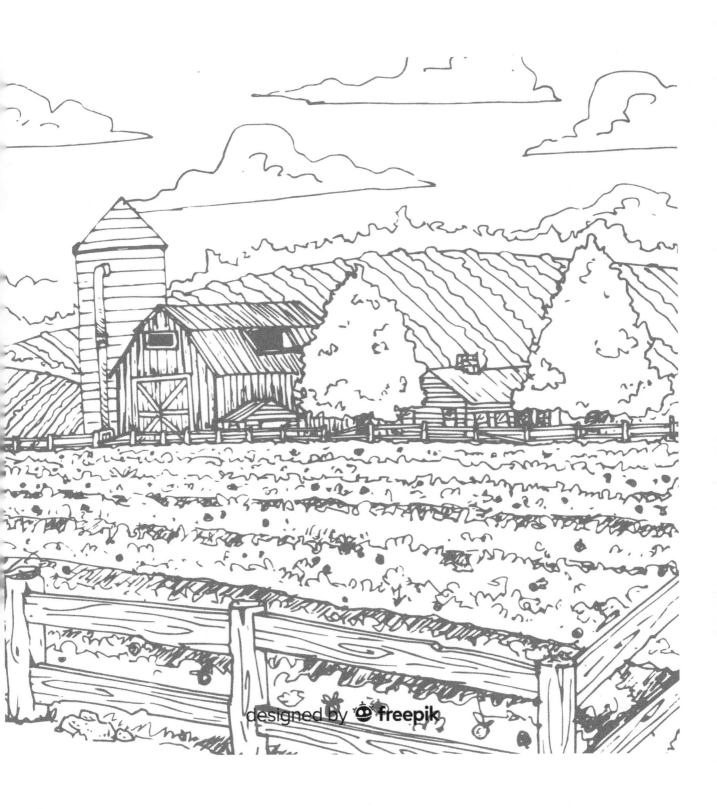

CPSIA information can be obtained
at www.ICGtesting.com
Printed in the USA
BVHW022101140423
662364BV00005B/176